The Single Woman's PRAYER BOOK

HOW TO GET ANSWERS FROM HEAVEN

SARITA A. FOXWORTH

Copyright © 2018 by Sarita A. Foxworth

All rights reserved. This book or any portion thereof may not be reproduced or used in any manner whatsoever without the express written permission of the publisher except for the use of brief quotations in a book review.

Printed in the United States of America

2 3 4 5 6 7 8 9 10

ISBN 978-1719312370

Published by The Single Woman's Bookstore

www.thesinglewomansbookstore.com

table of CONTENTS

Introduction: The Power of Prayer 1

Part 1: Creating and Elevating Your Prayer Life 5
    Chapter 1: Creating Your Prayer Life 7
    Chapter 2: Entering the Presence of God 11
    Chapter 3: Your Heavenly Prayer Language 17

Part 2: Hearing from God: Clarity and Confirmation 29
    Chapter 4: Four Ways to Hear from God 31
    Chapter 5; You were Created to Hear from God 41
    Chapter 6: Clarity and Confirmation: God's Timing 45
    Chapter 7: Clarity and Confirmation: The Five Checkpoints 51
    Chapter 8: Next Steps 61

Part 3: Prayers for Self and Future Husband 63
    Chapter 9: Topical Prayers 65
    Topical Prayers for the Phenomenal Single Woman 67
    Topical Intercessory Prayers for Future Husband 73

About the Author 79

Introduction
THE POWER OF PRAYER

When you have been single for a long time and desire to be married with children, you may have some questions you would love to have the answers to. Do any of these questions sound familiar?

- Why am I still single?
- Why did the last man or men hurt me?
- What is wrong with me?
- Have I done something wrong to still be single?
- When is my husband going to find me?
- What should my focus be during this season of singleness?
- How can I prepare for the husband God is sending me?

In addition to these questions you may also wonder what your life's purpose is, where you should serve in ministry, what's the next move you should make professionally or in your business, and where and when should you settle down. In other words, your heart needs answers to gain understanding of your current season and your mind needs clarity and direction when making life choices. This is the reason hearing from God is extremely important in your single season.

When you go home at night, you are alone with your thoughts. You have no husband to bounce things off of, goal set and make future plans with. You don't have a built-in prayer partner to agree with you on heart matters. However, as a child of God you do have the Holy Spirit. He is your Helper. He is your Comforter. He is your Guide. You should never have unanswered questions or lack of direction simply because you are unmarried. You should be able to go directly to the throne of God in your prayer, study and/or quiet time to gain the answers and insight you need.

Prayer is powerful. Not only because God's power is released to make miracles, signs and wonders possible, but because of the inward power that is released. And that power is at work on the inside of you. There is power that is released when you hear from God and submit to his leadership. At the place of obedience grace begins to flow. When he reveals his plans and purpose for your life, then your heart can move from a place of confusion and frustration to a place of hope and peace…that is a powerful experience. When you go to him and take your lonely thoughts and feelings of despair, and allow him to minister to your spirit, infuse you with his strength and give you a vision for your future, then the power of God is being released over your life. Praying is the most powerful thing you can do, coupled with submission to the will of God for your life.

Throughout these pages I want to help you begin to hear from God in a greater capacity. I want to help you enhance your prayer life in a way that you can bring your heart issues directly to God and gain insight, clarity, and direction for your single season. As you receive this teaching and guidance, I believe you will be able to flow with God, not only during times of planned prayer, but also in any moment when you need to hear the voice of God. Be encouraged, sis. As much as you want to hear from God, he wants you to hear from him. As much as you want answer, he wants to be the one to give them to you. Your heavenly Father wants you to come to him first, not your friends, not your mama, not your cousin, reality TV or social media. He wants to be the ultimate authority, guide, and comforter in your life.

If you are reading this book and you have not yet made Jesus the Lord of your life, you will not be able to access the presence of God in the capacity that I will describe. The first desire God has for your life is to be in fellowship with you. He wants to fill your spirit with his Spirit so that you can have a true relationship with him. In order for this to take place you must first give your heart to Christ by confessing Jesus as your Lord and Savior and receive His spirit into your heart. Most Christians call this experience a spiritual rebirth, or being "born again". You can receive Jesus as your Lord and Savior and experience this rebirth right now by saying the following prayer out loud:

> LORD, I AM READY TO GIVE MY HEART TO YOU.
> I BELIEVE THAT JESUS IS MY LORD AND SAVIOR.
> I BELIEVE IN THE SACRIFICE THAT HE MADE FOR
> MY SINS WHEN HE GAVE HIS LIFE ON THE CROSS
> AND ROSE ON THE THIRD DAY WITH ALL POWER.
> BEGIN TO SPEAK TO MY HEART, LEAD ME BY
> YOUR SPIRIT AND ALLOW ME TO EXPERIENCE YOUR
> PRESENCE AND LOVE LIKE NEVER BEFORE.
> IN JESUS' NAME, AMEN.

Now, you are ready to grow with God and go into deeper realms of his divine love for you.

PART 1

CREATING AND ELEVATING YOUR PRAYER LIFE

Chapter 1
CREATING YOUR PRAYER LIFE

Now that you have received Jesus as your Lord and Savior, or even if you are a seasoned saint, I want to give some information to help you create or elevate your prayer life. If you have been walking with the Lord for some time, some of this guidance and tips will sound basic, while other items will be new and refreshing. I encourage you to be open-minded and try what sounds like it will work for you. Everyone's prayer life looks different. What is important is that you are growing in your relationship with God and that you dedicate some time for just you and him to communicate, engage, and worship.

QUALITY TIME

First and foremost, you must set aside some quality time to spend in the presence of God. Everyone's schedule is different so what works best for you may not be the same as what works for someone else. Some women like to pray in the mornings to get the day started. This is an excellent option if you are able to make the time shortly after waking. You can start the day in the Word and in prayer with a cup of coffee and have a pleasant tone set right away. When you start your day hearing from God, it can make it easier to hear from Him throughout the day as well. Even though I do not start my day in prayer, I do say a simple prayer each morning and acknowledge the Holy Spirit so that He is immediately in my thoughts and involved with my early morning decisions.

You can choose to have prayer in the evening before you go to bed as well. What I like about winding down with the Lord, is I can reflect on my day and talk pressing issues on my heart over with God. This way I do not go to sleep stressed or feeling burdened by anything. It's like a sweet release while the Lord simultaneously fills me up with his peace, joy and love right before I rest my mind and body.

At times, I would use my lunch breaks for prayer, especially when fasting and praying about a matter. At one period of fasting and praying I had my own office and would use that 30 minutes to get on my knees and pray, instead of eating a meal. Those quiet worship moments in the middle of my workday would be extremely blessed as well. Even though it was a 30-minute prayer session, I got a lot out of them. This leads me to my next point: you don't always have to spend an hour or more in prayer. You decide what works best for your lifestyle and schedule. As long as you are making time for God daily, you will be able to spend lots of time with him on some days and on others have short worship sessions. God is not requiring you to pray an hour a day. He knows your schedule. He sees your effort. What is important is that you try and you make the time for God regularly.

SET YOUR ATMOSPHERE

You can set your prayer atmosphere in a few ways. I have also found that depending on what time of day and what location you have chosen to pray in or at, will also determine an effective way to set your atmosphere. For example, I used to have early morning prayer when I lived in high-rise in Atlanta. I would go out on my patio on the 14th floor that overlooked a park with the city in the horizon and sit with my coffee and my Word. The birds would be chirping, the cars would be the in background, but it was very peaceful. I would study, pray and start my day feeling great.

When I have prayer times in the evening, most times I set my atmosphere with praise and worship music. This helps when there are many distractions on your mind or if you "feel" that you really need an encounter with God. God doesn't need music to move supernaturally, but because we are human with emotions, the music can help usher us into the presence of God. The worship leaders help us to clear our thoughts and focus solely on the awesome glory of the Lord. The music I love the most during these times is sometimes called "soaking" music. It's worship music that allows you to soak in the presence of God.

However, any time of praise and worship where Jesus is being exalted will set your atmosphere very nicely.

ENHANCING YOUR PRAYER TIME

Make your prayer time as enjoyable as possible. If you find your prayer life growing stagnant, do something different to not only motivate yourself but to help you upgrade your prayer life and go even deeper with God. Take prayer tools and resources into His presence and make the environment comfortable and cozy. After all, you are spending time with your Heavenly Father. He loves you so much. How would you spend time with your natural father who loves you? You do things together that you enjoy. You can take not only a pen and paper, but also take your written visions, plans and goals, light some candles, lay out some plush floor pillows, grab a pretty and chic prayer journal with a matching pretty pen, print out a beautiful confession or affirmation that you have created for your season. You can also switch up your environment. Take a prayer walk outside and enjoy nature as you converse with the Lord. Right now I work close to the beach. Sometimes on my lunch break, I drive out to the water and have an oceanfront conversation with God, overlooking the beautiful blue and green waves, listening to the pigeons fight for crumbs on the sand. These are peaceful moments I have with the Lord, which I enjoy greatly. What comes to mind when you think of ways you can possibly enhance or elevate your prayer life?

NOTES, THOUGHTS AND REFLECTIONS

Always make time for Lord however busy you are in your life. Learn to put him first in every thing, every choice every work.

Chapter 2
ENTERING THE PRESENCE OF GOD

PRAISE AND WORSHIP

Your prayer life is inclusive of private and corporate praise and worship. The Lord can and will speak to you during both moments. While it is very important to pray in public during church services or events, this chapter will focus mostly on private praise and worship since that is the focus of this book.

During your personal prayer time, you should incorporate moments of praise, worship and honoring the Lord in addition to quiet moments when you can have heart-to-heart conversations with the Lord. There is no rulebook to how you incorporate praise, worship and intimate conversations with God into your prayer life, so do what works best for you. Make it work for your schedule, personality and environment. As long as you are having time to worship the Lord in addition to making requests and receiving spiritual insight, your prayer life will be blessed. You also do not have to only worship the Lord during your set prayer time. At any moment where your spirit feels led (and the environment is appropriate), you can praise and worship the Lord. I have found that when my spirit feels led into deep worship, sometimes only for a moment, the Lord is simultaneously receiving my praise and honor, while sending a message directly into my spirit. I have received many messages from heaven outside of my normal prayer time throughout my daily life. When you have a lifestyle of prayer, this will happen for you also.

> Enter into His gates with thanksgiving and a thank offering and into His courts with praise! Be thankful and say so to Him, bless and affectionately praise His name!

Psalm 100:4 Amplified Bible, Classic Edition (AMPC)

We should always enter the presence of God with thanksgiving and praise, both verbally and within our hearts. You may not have a full blown worship and praise session, yet starting off your prayer time with the simple phrase: "Thank you Lord…" is highly effective. He wants to hear our gratitude. The same way we want to be appreciated when we take care of people. There is always something to be thankful for with God. You may be in the middle of or leaving a rough season of heartbreak, frustration with relationships, impatience with your singleness or anything else that seems not to go as planned. Yet, still there is a reason to be thankful to God. That situation did not destroy you. God still loves you and has never left you. He still has provision for you right in this moment. You have an opportunity to have what I call a "Genesis Moment", that is a moment or morning where you decide to start fresh and create the life you want anew. Plus, you made it through that situation, you are making it through this season you are in and there is a blessed future in store for you in your "Promise Land".

PRAYER POSTURE

Let us therefore come boldly to the throne of grace, that we may obtain mercy and find grace to help in time of need.
Hebrews 4:16 New King James Version (NKJV)

Therefore let us [with privilege] approach the throne of grace [that is, the throne of God's gracious favor] with confidence and without fear, so that we may receive mercy [for our failures] and find [His amazing] grace to help in time of need [an appropriate blessing, coming just at the right moment].
Hebrews 4:16 Amplified Bible (AMP)

When you go into prayer requesting of or petitioning the Lord, you should not be fearful, hesitant or go merely from obligation. Because you know the Word, meaning you know his promises and because you know the Spirit of God, meaning you KNOW him intimately, you can go boldly in his presence, before the throne of grace and make your requests known. What is there to be afraid of? He can only say yes, no or wait. I believe fear most times stems from sin or guilt. However, you must remember that God is there in those sinful moments. He is there when you disobey him. He is there when you fall short and make a mistake. Yet, he is a loving Father, who still wants you to come to him in your time of want or need. God can help you perfectly. He can provide for your heart, spirit and natural circumstances perfectly, as only he can. He is the Alpha and the Omega. He created the heavens and the earth. He created you, sis. Therefore, he knows exactly what you need and want. When you come to him prayer, it gives him joy and he is able to do exceeding and abundantly above all that you can ask think or imagine.

FRUIT BEARING AND ANSWERED PRAYER

> You did not choose Me, but I chose you and appointed you that you should go and bear fruit, and that your fruit should remain, that whatever you ask the Father in My name He may give you.
>
> *John 15:16 New King James Version (NKJV)*

I am sure you are wondering why your future husband hasn't manifested yet. The answer lies in the heart of our Father. You can seek his face for every answer to your heart's questions. I believe and stand in faith on the scripture referenced above. We can truly ask the Father anything in Jesus' name and God will do it. However, the prerequisite in this scripture is also true. You must first be a fruit bearer. You were chosen for a specific plan, purpose and destiny. Do you know that not every person in history will receive salvation? Not every single person in the creation of the world will be saved. Yet, God has chosen you. I know he has chosen you because you are reading this book. You may have even said the introductory prayer of salvation at the beginning of this book for the first time. YOU, sis, have been chosen. You have been appointed. But what are you chosen and appointed to do? That answer again lies in the heart of your Father, but it is the key to purpose and fulfillment. There is something that you specifically have been designed and purposed to create and birth in the earth within this generation to which you have been born. Becoming a wife is a part of that purpose since you have the God given desire to be married. After all, not every single woman even wants to be married. Again, this is proof that you have been chosen and appointed to be single, but then later to shift seasons and become a wife.

The focus for your single season must be fruit bearing in every area of your life. Chase godly purpose and the Lord will connect you and your husband on the path of purpose. You and he are destined to become purpose partners. There is much work to do in the kingdom of God in fulfilling the great commission and leading others to Christ or into a deeper relationship with Christ in this hour. The fruit that your life bears accomplishes this mission. The Lord taught me years ago that different fruit speaks to different people. For example, one person can love how confident you are as a woman, while another person will be more drawn to the financial prosperity you have acquired. Both of these people need Jesus. And now, you have an open door to indirectly or directly lead them both to Christ because of the fruit that is seen on your life.

As you work on becoming the best version of yourself, fruit will abound in your life. You will grow spiritually, emotionally, intellectually and naturally. The foundation during the single season is being laid for your future life as a wife and mother. As you grow and build on that foundation with God, you will find that when it's time to pray for your husband and children you will know confidently that you can ask the Father in Jesus' name and He will do it!

NOTES, THOUGHTS AND REFLECTIONS

Chapter 3
YOUR HEAVENLY PRAYER LANGUAGE

Teaching the topic of prayer tongues can be daunting and intimidating to say the least (just being honest!), because of the negative implications perpetuating it within and outside of the Body of Christ. However, I cannot write a prayer book without addressing one the most powerful gifts I have personally experienced. That is, the Baptism of the Holy Spirit with the evidence of praying in tongues. I will refer to this experience as your Heavenly Prayer Language, Prayer Tongues or Praying in the Spirit throughout this chapter. I will teach about this gift as simply as possible. Any tool, revelation or gift that God gives us to better our lives should never be confusing, but they will always be supernatural. They should not be scary or weird, yet they should be life transforming. And, as the reoccurring theme of this book states, they will also accomplish two things: The Great Commission being fulfilled and the love of God being expressed through your life.

In this chapter I will guide you through exactly what prayer tongues is, why you should pray in tongues, how to obtain the gift of the Holy Spirit, and how to utilize your personal prayer language throughout your life practically as a Christian woman, as well as the type of results and changes you should expect from praying in your heavenly prayer language.

WHAT IS PRAYER TONGUES?

You can do an entire study into prayer tongues and the Baptism of the Holy Spirit but I have been instructed by the Lord to keep this simple as possible and I shall oblige. I will give biblical basis and practical application in addition to my own personal experiences to teach this topic. If at any point you need greater revelation, take a moment and pray. Ask God for understanding and enlightenment. He will give it to you.

> And when Paul had laid hands on them, the Holy Spirit came upon them, and they spoke with tongues and prophesied.
> *Acts 19:6 New King James Version (NKJV)*

==Prayer tongues are the evidence that you have received the Baptism of the Holy Spirit.== Just as you can get baptized in water, you can also be baptized with the Holy Spirit. I will parallel this experience with salvation to make it easy to follow. When you receive salvation the Holy Spirit dwells within your spirit. When you are baptized with the Holy Spirit, the Spirit of God comes upon your spirit…and he stays there. You know for sure that his has taken place because you can now pray in tongues. Those who cannot pray in tongues have not received this baptism or do not believe in prayer tongues. You have to believe in order to receive this gift, just like you have to believe in Christ in order to receive salvation.

The Gift	How to Receive	What Happens	Evidence of Receipt	Scriptural Basis
Salvation	Belief and Verbal Confession	Holy Spirit dwells within your spirit	Expressed Faith in Christ and the Word	Roman 10:9-10
Baptism of the Holy Spirit	Belief and Ask God	Holy Spirit comes upon your spirit	Heavenly Prayer Language/Prayer Tongues	Acts 19:6, Acts 10:45-48

WHY PRAY IN TONGUES?

Your Heavenly prayer language is an amazing gift from God, I consider an additional layer of power for successful living here on this earth. When Jesus left to be seated at the right hand of the Father in Heaven he knew that we would still need his help here on earth. He knew that his presence would still be needed for wisdom, guidance, comfort, healing, miracles, power, and having a direct connection to the heart of

God. These are all the things he did himself when he walked the earth with us. His physical presence was the link to the Almighty Father in Heaven. When he left, he didn't leave us on our own, resorting back to methods of old—only having specific priests and prophets that could hear from and access the Spirit of God. He gave us the Holy Spirit so that we could not only have our own personal relationship with God, but also access all the power, strength, grace and might directly from heaven as individual followers of Christ. Once we receive the Baptism of the Holy Spirit, we ignite this power and put this power to work by releasing it through prayer tongues, which is our personal Heavenly Prayer Language.

The Lord always wants us to speak in order to release his will. We are following in his example throughout the Word. In Genesis, he spoke the earth into creation. When we pray, we have to say out loud what is on our hearts. He tells us in the Bible in the book of Proverbs that the tongue can bring life and death. When Jesus did any miracle in the synoptic gospels, he always spoke words. There is power in our words. When he engaged in spiritual warfare where he overcame temptation in the wilderness, he spoke to Satan and he fled. Our spoken words are powerful.

It is the same principle at work when we release the miracle working power of God when we pray in our Heavenly Prayer language. Here is what the Bible says will happen:

You are strengthened in your moment of weakness

> In the same way the Spirit [comes to us and] helps us in our weakness. We do not know what prayer to offer or how to offer it as we should, but the Spirit Himself [knows our need and at the right time] intercedes on our behalf with sighs and groanings too deep for words.
>
> *Romans 8:26 Amplified Bible (AMP)*

You grow in confidence in God

> While they were praying, the place where they were meeting trembled and shook. They were all filled with the

Holy Spirit and continued to speak God's Word with fearless confidence.

Acts 4:31 The Message (MSG)

You build your faith

But you, beloved, building yourselves up on your most holy faith, praying in the Holy Spirit,

Jude 20 New King James Version (NKJV)

You flow in the supernatural power of God

He who believes and is baptized will be saved; but he who does not believe will be condemned. And these signs will follow those who believe: In My name they will cast out demons; they will speak with new tongues; they[a] will take up serpents; and if they drink anything deadly, it will by no means hurt them; they will lay hands on the sick, and they will recover."

Mark 16:16-18 New King James Version (NKJV)

As single women of God we need all the supernatural help we can get. We need the Holy Spirit to give us strength, confidence, faith, and power. I can not imagine my life would be as it is today if I had not received this gift and began praying regularly in my prayer language following Paul's expressed example in 1 Corinthians 14:18.

HOW DO YOU OBTAIN THIS GIFT?

I want to reiterate the gift I am referring to is the gift of the Holy Spirit, not the gift of tongues. There is a difference between receiving the gift of the Holy Spirit by being baptized with The Spirit and then praying in tongues as evidence of this gift, and having the actual Gift of tongues. The Bible talks about three types of tongues and I am going to make it simple for you, so you can locate yourself and elevate your personal prayer life.

DEFINITIONS

The Gifts

1. **Gift of the Holy Spirit** - The Holy Spirit that Jesus sent when he went to heaven with Father God. The Holy Spirit came to us on earth first in the book of Acts Chapter 2. When he came, the people immediately began speaking in prayer tongues and tongues of other languages. Purpose of this gift-to help us as Jesus did when he was here, bequeath of power, personal spiritual edification, personal direct connection with God.

2. **Gift of Tongues** - A spiritual gift to the church that manifests as the Spirit of God wills in a corporate environment which requires corporate interpretation as well as stated in 1 Corinthians Chapter 14. When this gift is in operation at church, the gift of interpretation must immediately follow. The purpose of this gift is to release a prophetic Word of the Lord to an assembly of believers in corporate environment, which could be at church or an event.

Side note: The Gift of Tongues and interpretation are given by God as he wills in a corporate environment. You can ask to be used by God in this way, just like you can ask him to use you as a vessel to administer the gifts of healings, miracles, and prophecy. If God chooses to use you in this way, it will be for the benefit of believers and unbelievers. Remember, the Great Commission and love of God are always the end goal. However, we each have the option to receive the Gift of the Holy Spirit if we believe and ask for the manifestation of this gift, which will be our own personal prayer language of prayer tongues.

Types of Tongues

1. **Prayer Tongues** - AKA Heavenly Prayer Language, is a manifestation that is the evidence you have received the gift of the Baptism of the Holy Spirit. Used for personal benefit during private prayer.

2. **Tongues of Another Language** - manifestation of the Holy Spirit as he wills as a sign to benefit unbelievers. Unbelievers will view this manifestation as a miracle and a sign from God, that you can speak their language, even though you have not learned it through traditional means or methods.

3. **Corporate Tongues** - AKA Gift of Tongues is a manifestation of the Spirit of God used for prophecy when interpreted to an assembly of believers and must have an interpreter, which can be the same person or other prophets within that assembly. Used only during corporate worship services at church or at an event to benefit that group of believers and unbelievers publicly.

PRAYING IN YOUR OWN HEAVENLY PRAYER LANGUAGE

Now that you have a deeper understanding on the surface level of what the gift of the Baptism of the Holy Spirit is and why it is important to pray in tongues for your own personal benefit, I want to help you receive this gift and start praying in tongues today. It is not weird or spooky. Nothing crazy is going to happen, yet something supernatural will absolutely take place. Remember, God is supernatural and he has created us to flow with His Spirit in a supernatural way. But God has not made anything too complex for us to receive from him and flow in our daily lives.

Here is a simply three-step process to receive the gift and pray in your own heavenly prayer language today:

Step 1) Believe.
Read the scriptures referenced in this chapter and/or listen to sermons taught by Kenneth Hagin, Kenneth Claytor and/or Creflo Dollar. Those helped me the most during my initial learning period, but I received the gift after hearing the teachings of Kenneth Claytor directly. Faith comes by hearing the Word of God taught. Practical teaching on this topic that is birthed from a place of love will help you the most, as it has done for me personally.

Step 2) Ask.
It's that simple. Ask God to baptize you with the gift of the Holy Spirit with the evidence of prayer tongues. He will honor your faith request in that moment. The Bible gives examples of believers receiving this gift by the laying on of hands. However, this is not a requirement in each instance. Some instances the Holy Spirit came and baptized everyone in the room without anyone asking, at other times a minister of the gospel taught individuals one-on-one and they received the gift by hearing and believing, or having faith. Romans 4:16 tells us that all

the promises of God are received by faith.

Step 3) Pray out loud.

Open your mouth and begin to pray effortlessly. The groanings and utterings that flow from you, this is your heavenly prayer language. The Lord will not force you to pray in tongues. He will not take over your body and make you pray. This would be weird and some type of spiritual possession, which is demonic. God does not force us to do anything. He does not force us to pray, love him, live according to his word, or anything else, he allows us to do whatever we want with our lives and in our bodies. And nothing should take over your body . You pray with your own will and your own voice box. Your participation and attempt to pray confirms what you believe in your heart and it begins to flow out of your mouth, out of your spirit and this will be your Heavenly Prayer Language.

MY STORY

When I received this gift with the evidence of prayer tongues, I responded to an alter call after a powerful teaching about the gift. After I went to the front of the church, those of us who were there were taken back and we reviewed a few scriptures, prayed, and then the prayer leader laid hands on everyone in the room so that we could receive the gift. Then there was a moment for the manifestation to take place. We were supposed to open our mouths and begin to pray, allowing our prayer tongues to flow from our spirits. I opened my mouth but looked around, wondering what they meant. I continued to stare at others praying in their Heavenly Prayer Language, the time was up and it was time to go back into the sanctuary. I didn't have my Prayer Language though, but I still wanted to. We were encouraged pray as much as possible and pray in our personal prayer time. I followed those exact instructions.

When I went home that evening I had my normal prayer time. I opened up with praise and worship music and singing to God while giving him thanks. Then I asked God about prayer tongues. I asked him why it hadn't manifested, and asked for his help, because I wanted the manifestation of this gift I believe I had already received. I wanted the power of God upon my life, I wanted to access Jesus in an elevated manner to have transformation on my life. I believe, my faith and desire wanted it so bad, it was not hard for me to receive. As I was having those thoughts of how I wanted the gift so badly and how my life would benefit from the gift, my Heavenly Prayer language started to flow out of me, effortlessly. All I did was open my mouth and focus on God. I focused on the promise and gift of the Holy Spirit and all that the Word said about the benefits. I started off praying slowly a few syllables at a time. Minutes later, the prayer began to flow in full sentences and paragraphs. My life was transformed from that moment forward and I have been extremely blessed ever since.

PRACTICALLY PRAYING IN THE SPIRIT

Your life as a follower of Christ should be supernatural. You should do things and operate differently than those who do not know Christ. You should also be experiencing different results in your single season than those women who are single and without a relationship with Christ. You have an advantage over them, which should help lead them to Christ as they see the fruit which your single season bears. You have the option to pray and hear from God immediately. You also have an additional layer of power when you pray in the Spirit using your Heavenly Prayer Language. You can grow in faith and confidence, release power into your situation and build your spirit up, praying for things you don't even know you need, but God does. You should pray during your prayer time in the Spirit as well as throughout your day as needed. Don't be weird or spooky about it in front of other people. After all it is personal prayer between you and God.

Here is a brief list of moments when you should pray, in addition to adding a few minutes to your prayer time:

- When you need to make a decision
- When you need to hear from God in that moment
- When you need the circumstance to change in a way that will glorify God
- When you feel helpless or hopeless
- When you feel weary
- When you need a miracle

- When you don't know what to do

- When you are stressed

- When you feel like you are out of control, mentally or emotionally

- When you are interceding for your future husband, family, friends and colleagues

WHAT PRAYER TONGUES IS NOT

Once you begin praying regularly in the Spirit it will be such a normal part of your life, you will pray automatically when your mind and heart need guidance or rest. As with many of the items I teach in this book, remember that I am not talking about anything strange, scary or weird. This is not a prayer language that will invoke spirits or control God or other people. That is impossible. No matter how convincing the counterfeit spirits of Satan may seem, it is not real and does not lead to good. Deception is supposed to look and feel good, while leading people to death. Praying in tongues is for your own personal spiritual benefit and helps your life to glorify God. The two foundational principles that will still apply here are: The Great Commission being fulfilled and God's love being the root and outcome of this experience.

For every good thing that God creates, Satan has created a counterfeit to confuse believers and nonbelievers. The counterfeit's power is rooted in deception. Once a person is deceived, the counterfeit appears to be real. It appears to really work, really be good, or really be God. However, this is not true. Satan is the father of lies, and his counterfeit spirits are a part of his lies. You can discern counterfeits the same way you can confirm whether God's voice is speaking to you or not. Prayer tongues follows the same confirmation process. There are counterfeit prayer tongues in operation within religious sectors that do not acknowledge Jesus as Lord and Savior. You can tell a counterfeit because the control and power starts from within that person and not from the spirit of God. While God does use our bodies as vessels of his spirit as the feet and hands of Jesus, the goal is always the same, leading others to Christ or into a closer relationship with Christ, and administering God's love. Counterfeit spirits are about tapping into some ungodly supernatural arena to fulfill a selfish desire that is not of God. It does not begin or end with Christ.

Sometimes, well-intentioned Christians cast prayer tongues in a negative light because they do not appropriate prayer tongues correctly. Here are two examples of how prayer tongues should not look. One woman was believing God for a new car. She goes to the dealership with a bottle of oil, splashes it all over the car she wants and prays in tongues loudly as she claims this car as her own. What do you think others who witness this behavior are thinking? I can tell you what they are not thinking. Wow, look at her faith, she is a true believer and follower of Christ, I want to be more like her! Wow, look at God working in her life. He is a miracle working, good God I want to know more about. Nope, these are not the thoughts of onlookers. If anything, they would think she is crazy and never go to the church she invites them to.

The second example is a woman who notices ungodly behavior from her brother. When she sees him, she lays hands on his head, prays in tongues, and tries to cast the devil out of him. Again, what do you think this woman's brother is going to think about her? I can tell you he is not thinking that his sister is so anointed and hears from God. He is going to first be offended that she said he had a devil in him, and he would think she was strange in her behavior and probably doing some type of witchcraft when she prays in tongues over him. God will not be glorified in either of these situations.

Consider a woman who believes God for a car. She should pray during her prayer time in tongues so God can give her wisdom and strategies on how to organize her finances or even lead her to the person she has favor with in making the car deal. When she is feeling stressed or doubting, in that moment she should pray under her breath in her prayer language until she senses the peace of God come upon her spirit. In this same way, the woman I mentioned earlier should intercede for her brother in her private prayer time using her Heavenly Prayer Language on his behalf. The Lord can answer her prayers and move on his spirit as he wills, and he can also provide her with wisdom on how to love her brother better to reach his soul for Christ. Notice in both of these examples, the women should pray in private, then make godly moves in public and give God glory as a testimony of his goodness. This is how you practically pray in the Spirit throughout your daily life.

NOTES, THOUGHTS AND REFLECTIONS

PART 2

HEARING FROM GOD: CLARITY AND CONFIRMATION

Chapter 4
FOUR WAYS TO HEAR FROM GOD

There are four ways that God can and may speak to you to reveal his Will, plans, purpose, desires, or give direction for your life. His presence also provides love, comfort, joy and peace as needed. The way God chooses to speak to you is personal communication that you will receive as you seek the Lord and grow in your relationship with Him. You may or may not hear from God in all four ways because God will speak to you in your own special way. Rest assured that you can get to a point in your relationship with God that when he speaks you will know it is his Spirit guiding you. When in doubt, however, there are five ways to confirm what you have received from the Lord, which I will discuss later. For now, I will share four Biblical ways God you can hear from God with examples of how he has spoken to me at various moments in my life.

As I describe the ways in which God can speak remember, these three very important things:

1) **God is love.** Everything that God does is going to be rooted in and driven by love. The end result will also be a love bearing action or result, whether that is a self-love or loving others. The greatest commandment the Lord gave us, was to love others as we love ourselves. When the Lord speaks, it is always going to be coming from a loving place. Even though the corresponding actions from what you hear may not please others, you cannot please everyone. The plans of God are love-based and governed.

2) **We serve a supernatural God.** Each way to hear from God is based on scripture. None of these ways are strange or spooky. They are not over the top. Everything we believe as Christians is based on

faith, those things we cannot see. The Bible has story after story of supernatural occurrences. Our lives should also flow with God and we should live supernatural, blessed lives just like the men and women we read about in scripture. Our greatest example, is the supernatural life of our King of Kings, the Lord Jesus Christ.

3) You can not control how or when God speaks to you. The Lord chooses how he wants to communicate with you based on circumstances and how he desires to speak to you in that specific moment. I am not teaching about anything that originates in our human mind or efforts. We pray when we speak with God about what is on our hearts, or as we intercede for others. However, we can not dictate how and when God responds. You can rest assured that he will respond, but how he responds is not in your control.

Let's get into the four ways that you can hear from God. You may or may not hear from God in all four ways. The Lord will decide how he speaks to you, depending on the situation and what he wills in that specific moment.

1. HIS STILL SMALL VOICE

Scripture Reference: 1 Kings 19:12 (NKJV)

When you hear people speak of hearing the voice of God, we are speaking about the still small voice the Bible speaks of in the scripture reference above. It is not an audible voice; it is not a scary voice. And it is not a weird sounding voice that causes us to feel frightened or uneasy. The still small voice of God is one our spirit recognizes, it is not a foreign voice. The Lord tell us in his Word that "My sheep know My voice". Our spirits will recognize the voice of God and this voice will bare witness in our inner most being, that is, within our own spirits.

Since the voice of God is so familiar with our spirits, sometimes it can be hard to tell whether it is God's voice or our own thoughts running through our minds. Also, since our enemy is a counterfeit spirit, he tries to disguise himself as the voice of God and lead us astray. It is very important that we can differentiate between God's voice, our voice, and the voice of the enemy. Don't worry, this isn't as difficult as it may sound.

I will give you more details and examples of how to tell when you are truly hearing the voice of God, but I want to get you started with a foundational method for discerning the voice of God. One day I was praying and I simply asked God to tell me how I could tell the difference between his voice, my voice, and the voice of the enemy. He told me, "Because my voice will always contain love and authority." I understood exactly what he was telling me in that moment. God is love. Not only would the information he would be telling me come from a place of love, be rooted in love and also lead to love filled actions and decisions, but I would also be able to "sense" his love. The love of God is so much greater than an emotional feeling of love, yet that is a part of how his presence manifest for us. His love is all consuming, gentle, peaceful, fulfilling and filled with joy. Therefore, if the voice you hear is telling you to do something that will lead you on the opposite path of love (whether it's loving others or loving yourself) or away from the Word, it is not God. If the voice you are hearing is leading you to take an action that will lead to hurt, strife, unrest or have negative consequences, it is not God. Don't misunderstand me, sometimes we have to make hard decisions and God leads us to take actions that others may not like. Yet the end result will always be peace and love, self-love and/or loving others. After all, the greatest commandment is to love others as we love ourselves.

There are many examples throughout the old and new testaments of men and women of God hearing and being led by the still small voice of God. Each story is not identical, however each time the Lord spoke it was for a godly purpose. As Spirit-filled believers, we should be able to hear from God each time we pray. Prayer should be a two-way dialogue, not a one-way monologue. What better way could there be for God to direct your footsteps and be a lamp unto your path, than to reveal his desires and guidance to you in prayer. Yes, you can and should hear from God, speaking directly to your heart on a regular basis.

2. DISCERNMENT

Scripture Reference 2 Corinthians 5:11 (AMP); Proverbs 4:7 (AMP)

Spiritual discernment is what most of us call a "woman's intuition" but I believe it is much greater than just a hunch or a feeling. God can show you mysteries that can only be revealed using your "spiritual eyes". In other words, you can pick up on things transpiring in the spiritual realm using your heart and spirit. This is not weird or spooky. I am not talking about anything within human control, which would be witchcraft or sorcery. I am also not talking about anything that would scare you or someone else. However, I am talking about something supernatural. As a follower of Christ, we should live supernatural lives. Most of the things that we believe and trust in concerning the Lord Jesus Christ is supernatural. Not strange, not weird and not scary. The Lord is the revealer of everything you discern as a believer. You don't determine what is and what is not revealed, it is in accordance to the will of God in that moment or circumstance and will always be for his glory. Remember, God is love. When we flow in the supernatural with God, it will be founded and rooted in love, and the end results will produce a love based action. You cannot control what you discern because God is the revealer of these mysteries, not us. When God speaks to you in this way and reveals something to you, just as his voice is rooted, grounded, and intended for love, so will your spiritual discernment operate in a similar way.

When I first began dating an ex-boyfriend I will refer to as "The Good Deacon", at the end of our very first date the Lord spoke to me through spiritual discernment. After dinner when he walked me to my car, we stood outside chatting for a few minutes. Then, as he spoke it was as if my spiritual eyes were open. I could see through his chest and beyond the physical body. It was not an X-ray type of vision, there was a seeing and a sensing at the same time. I could "feel" sadness and yearning simultaneously surrounding and infusing his heart, consuming the entirety of his chest area. I could literally see and sense this pain at the same time, as he was making small talk with me as we were departing. The Lord was revealing the emotional state of The Good Deacon in this very moment.

Later, I asked him if he was sad about anything. He told me no. I wasn't surprised when he didn't express his true feelings to me. It could have been because our relationship was too new to share deep feelings early on, or because he was in denial. I knew that the Lord was warning me about his emotional state for my own protection. I should not have gotten close to the deacon because his heart was not in the proper condition to fully love me. He was not whole emotionally or spiritually. At the end of our short-lived relationship, he admitted to me that he was not ready to give of himself fully to any woman, because he was still hurting from the pain he endured from his 17-year marriage, which ended due to infidelity. Although I tried to convince myself that I could pray him through his pain and be there to love him despite his hurting, the disobedience to my own discernment landed me with a relationship full of confusion, deceit, and hurt feelings.

This was not the Lord's will for me. To be hurt and deceived while trying to love a man is not God's desire for my life or yours. The love God has for me caused him to attempt to warn me, as he does with you also at times. I should have listened. When the Lord reveals things to you by his Spirit, the best response is to ask him in prayer how best to move forward then submit and obey his leadership. If you ignore your discernment, you will only end up hurt and sometimes battling regret and self-forgiveness because you made the wrong decision. Rest assured, however, that you can get back on track after a season of disobedience. The Lord is willing and waiting for you to have a "Genesis" moment, a new and fresh beginning with greater wisdom and understanding.

3. A WORD OF WISDOM OR WORD OF KNOWLEDGE

Scripture Reference: 1 Corinthians 12:8 (AMP)

The best way that I can describe the Lord using a Word of Wisdom or Word of Knowledge to speak to you is that a word, phrase or even paragraph can drop in your spirit during your prayer time or as you go about your daily life. The first time I had this experience I was praying about a matter in my prayer time and studying the Word on the matter. As I listened for the still small voice to give me guidance, I received more than my usual sentence or phrase. I received an entire chapter of information in a split second. I was caught off guard because normally when the Lord speaks to me, I hear words rolled out as if we are having a person to person conversation. I had never received a large amount of information; a knowing in my spirit in a moment.

I wanted to make sure I was understanding what was being revealed so I asked the Lord, what just happened. I asked him if he could slow down the rate of what he was telling me about, instead of giving me the whole chapter of information at once, could he speak slowly to me so that I would know it was him leading me in that moment. He assured me right then that it was indeed His spirit speaking me and that for me, this was another level of answered prayer. He told me that at times he would begin to speak to me this way, by dropping a Word of knowledge or a Word of wisdom into my spirit. He would at times give me a large amount of information, a full and detailed vision, instruction or teaching in a split second of human time.

As a Spirit filled and Spirit-led woman of God, you may at times feel as if you "just know" something. Again, this information will be delivered from heaven, therefore it is not in your control, but in accordance with God's will. I am not referring to anything a medium, spiritist or psychic claims to have knowledge of. I am talking about a supernatural revelation given by God for the sake of leading souls to Christ or into a closer relationship with Christ. Everything that is revealed not only will be predicated on love, but will lead directly or indirectly to the Great Commission being fulfilled. The Lord will not give you purposeless information or insight that would cause dissention, deception, confusion or judgement to take place. Sometimes deception can feel like it is love when someone claims to have spiritual insight and knowledge that appears to comfort and be helpful. Yet, the Bible warns us about false spirits, spirits of error and witchcraft/sorcery spirits. If the "spirit" does not confess Jesus as Lord and Savior, it is a counterfeit spirit. No matter how good is appears or feels, the end result will not be love bearing or Great Commission fulfilling. God is love and his first priority is the salvation of souls to increase the family he desires so very much, the family of God which is the Body of Christ.

4. VISIONS AND DREAMS

Scripture Reference: Joel 2:28 (NKJV)

Visions and dreams from can be very powerful, yet can also be confusing if not interpreted or used correctly. I am a dreamer and have had dreams almost nightly my entire life. When I experienced a supernatural transformation in my spirit, a rededication to Christ, I was on fire for God and full of zest and zeal. I thought every dream that I had, had a deep biblical or spiritual meaning. I was buying dream interpretation books, seeking out other dream and vision having women in the body of Christ, planning to attend dream workshops and seminars, all in the hopes of finding greater understanding for the dreams I was having. When I asked leaders in my church about my dreams, some would try to loosely interpret them, others would tell me to pray about it. I felt like I had a gift that was not being recognized or developed. So I looked outside of the ministry for help. Also, with a pure heart, I thought that every dream I had about someone else was for me to share with them so that they could receive the message God was trying to deliver through me. My intentions were good, yet my guidance was off.

It is true that God can give you a vision or dream for yourself or to help someone else. However, not all dreams or visions come from God. Sometimes they are simply our own emotions being expressed in a sleeping state or even birthed from our imagination. Our imagination can be powerful. When we are sleeping our imagination mixed with our emotions can create some very convincing and intense dreams. How many times have you had a dream that something bad was happening and you woke up in tears or your heart racing or upset about what transpired during your sleeping state.

The best wise council that I received from my pastor at the time was to ask God to tell me what the dreams meant before I ran with them. Before you try to research on Google or in a dream book, or ask someone else to interpret for you, your first stop should be the presence of God. He will tell you if the dream was in fact a message from heaven or not. Whether the dream was good or bad, about you or about someone else, always ask God first to tell you if it was from him or not. If it was a message from him, he will then instruct you on how to move forward with what he has shown you. Just like the other ways that God speaks, dreams and visions will always be predicated on love, lead to love based actions and results and fulfill the Great Commission.

Therefore, if God in fact does give you a dream or a vision, the next step will be to gain further direction from the Lord on how to proceed. He doesn't want to confuse you with a dream or vision. If the message causes confusion, it is not from God. God is not the author of confusion. He wants to be the lamp unto your footsteps. How can he enlighten your path, if he causes you to be confused? He wants to direct your footsteps. So a message from him will have instructions included. I have found that I have gotten a vision just to confirm something taking place in my life personally that I was praying about or perhaps when God wants to reveal something greater than what I am thinking or considering in the moment. He has given me dreams for a specific direction in my own life when I needed a clear answer or plan, and he gave me a visual representation of what was to come as the outcomes of my decisions because it was the best way to communicate with me for that situation.

When God has given me dreams concerning others, not once has it been for me to go to them and express what God has shown me. It has always been for me to intercede for them, pray for their current state, protection, situation or future, or to reach out them or minister to them more effectively. Although I have not had personal experiences speaking to someone about what has been revealed to me, I do believe it is possible. There are many biblical stories when dreams are given to be shared with the person it was about. However, God will instruct you to do so. Taking it upon yourself to speak into someone's life can do more harm than good, even though your intentions are in the right place. They may not be ready for what you are planning to share with them and will shut you out. You may be speaking about something God has shown in the future for you to pray about presently and when you tell the person and it doesn't manifest right away, now you and God look like liars. Plus, that person may not be open to receiving any type of God-given word from you. If they do respect your anointing, you can cause them to also get outside of the will of God by getting ahead of themselves and focusing on a future that it is not meant for them to prepare for presently. The Lord may want you to simply pray for that person's future, not reveal it. He will want them to seek God in their own personal prayer lives and gain insight into their own future for themselves.

If you have a dream or vision that is a nightmare, devastating or very negative for you or someone else, the best thing you can do for that person or for yourself is pray. The most powerful thing you can do is pray and confess the Word of God over their life and/or yours. Find scriptures pertaining to god's covering and covenant, long life, angelic protection, the blood of Jesus, the Lord's strength and might and speak those scriptures out loud. Depending on what the dream or vision was about, do a topical search to find scriptures that oppose the negativity and decree God's promises over the situation.

Lastly, just like the other ways God may speak to you, you can not control if and when God gives you a vision or dream. However, you can ask for one pertaining to your own future and I do believe God will give you one. You can not control the details of how and if it happens, but if you go to God sincerely desiring for him to reveal his plans, purpose and vision for your own life, he will show you. These types of dream and visions are given to encourage your heart and stir up your faith. Yet, you must still gain specific instruction of how to move forward with what you believe you have received visually from the Lord.

NOTES, THOUGHTS AND REFLECTIONS

Chapter 5
YOU WERE CREATED TO HEAR FROM GOD

I want to encourage you that the ways I have spoken about in which you can hear from God are not just for special and highly anointed men and women of God. You do not need a church title or ordination to have a close and intimate relationship with God, so close that he can speak to you in the small and great things in life. No one needs to lay hands on you in order for you to receive a dream or vision from God. No one needs to give you permission to receive a Word of Wisdom or Word of knowledge from God. We each can flow with the Spirit of God as believers, at any given time that the Lord sees fit. God is not looking for those with titles to use. He looks for willing hearts. The Word of God tells us that the manifestation of the Spirit is given to each one of us to profit us all. In other words, when God speaks to you, you can now help yourself so that you can help others shortly thereafter. The Lord will speak to you about your single season, so that you can fulfill purpose and become the Proverbs 31 woman you were specifically created to become. `

As children of the Most High God, we are prophetic people. You should live your life as a supernatural woman of God, operating with much wisdom, understanding, and love. Your ways may be hard for the carnal minded, but for the kingdom minded people in the Body of Christ, it should be normal practice to hear from God and gain answers directly from heaven on a regular basis. You should never need to consult a medium or psychic for answers about your present or future seasons. You have the Spirit of the one, true living God on the inside of you to lead and guide you. As a matter of fact, other women of God should come to you to help them hear from God, interpret dreams, and make God-led decisions in their lives. You should flow with God and teach others to flow with God.

Additionally, once God sends you the husband you have been praying for, you can be the best helpmeet for him when you are able to get answers direct from heaven. You will need to intercede for him when he is stressed or burdened with his leadership responsibilities. God will tell you exactly how to pray for him. You will need to hear from God concerning what decisions to make together in your household. When it comes to raising and training your children, hearing from God is essential to raising up God fearing children of God. Not only will God speak to you about how to raise them and teach them the hard lessons of life, but there will be times when you need godly wisdom to protect your children, and even your husband. If you are struggling to hear from God pertaining to your own life and decisions as a single woman, more stress will be in your future if you do not know how to discern God's leadership once more is added to your care, like marriage and children. This can lead to you becoming overwhelmed trying to learn God's voice and figure out what you are hearing and how to pray, while also trying to teach your children to pray and hear from God or come into agreement with your husband on a family matter you may disagree on when instead, the Lord may have the precise wisdom to bring peace and unity in your home.

You were created to have a close relationship with God. It is not difficult for you to begin hearing from his Spirit once you are committed to do so. Below is a daily prayer for you to pray over the next seven days straight during your new or enhanced prayer time. I have also included some space for you to write out your thoughts and what you believe God is beginning to reveal or speak to you over the next seven days. You can also pair this book with The Single Woman's Prayer Journal to keep track of prayers over the next 52 weeks. Remember, God's word comes to direct, teach, comfort, build, encourage and give understanding. God is not the author of confusion. As much as you want to hear from him, he wants you to receive your answers directly from heaven as well. As you begin to document what the Lord is saying to you, it will become clearer and your relationship with God will grow.

The Single Woman's Prayer

FATHER,
I PRAY THAT YOU WILL BEGIN TO SPEAK TO MY HEART IN THIS SEASON LIKE NEVER BEFORE. MAKE MY SPIRIT SENSITIVE TO YOUR SPIRIT AND HELP ME TO RECEIVE YOUR LEADERSHIP AND GUIDANCE FOR MY SINGLE SEASON. SHOW ME WHAT YOU WOULD HAVE ME TO FOCUS ON DURING THIS SEASON SO THAT I MAY GROW SPIRITUALLY, EMOTIONALLY, MENTALLY, AND NATURALLY. REVEAL TO ME THE PURPOSE FOR WHICH YOU HAVE CREATED ME, SO THAT I MAY BEGIN TO FOCUS AND FLOW IN THIS PURPOSE. I THANK YOU FOR PREPARING MY FUTURE HUSBAND FOR ME, AS YOU PREPARE ME FOR HIM. GIVE ME AN ABUNDANCE OF WISDOM FOR DATING AND STARTING NEW FRIENDSHIPS WITH MEN. HELP ME NOT TO RUSH OR BE ANXIOUS BUT TO GET TO KNOW THEM IN THE DATING/ COURTING PROCESS WHILE LISTENING FOR YOUR LEADERSHIP ALONG THE WAY. GIVE ME STRENGTH AND THE SPIRIT OF OBEDIENCE TO SUBMIT TO YOUR GUIDANCE AND LEADERSHIP THROUGHOUT THIS SEASON. REMOVE ALL CONFUSION AND CLUTTER THAT WOULD TRY TO DETER ME FROM YOUR PERFECT WILL.
IN JESUS' NAME, AMEN.

NOTES & THOUGHTS

Day 1

Day 2

Day 3

Day 4

Day 5

Day 6

Day 7

Chapter 6
CLARITY AND CONFIRMATION: GOD'S TIMING

When you hear from God at times you may struggle with clarity-being clear about exactly what God has spoken or shown you and confirmation-being absolutely sure that the Lord has spoken to you. It is highly important that you have both clarity and confirmation when hearing from God, especially when making decisions that could change the course of your life or impact the lives of others. Major decisions such as what move to make professionally, in business, investments, relationships, ministry, family interactions, and/or how to move forward after a major life shift require clarity and confirmation. You have one, precious life to live. Although the Lord does not expect you to live a perfect life, he does expect you to try your best and be led of him so that His will for your life can be fulfilled.

As I go over five checkpoints to gain clarity and confirmation of what God has spoken, keep in mind two caveats. One, we walk by faith and not by sight, so it is okay to misunderstand or misinterpret here or there. Grace is here to catch us in our mistakes. Second, this is not a complicated process. God is not the author of confusion, so it is not hard to receive actual and clear answers from heaven on a regular basis.

I am going to use a personal experience as an example of how I walked myself through these five checkpoints when making a major life decision, purchasing my second home. When I purchased my first home, I didn't have a relationship with God and therefore did not consult him when making the purchase. I made a lot of compromises in order to stick to my budget. Even though it wasn't the desire of my heart, it checked off most of the boxes. However, the items I compromised on were not minor compromises, but were drastically below what I really wanted. Yet, I settled because I felt it was the best I could do. I knew nothing about praying, seeking God for guidance and favor, staying in faith and accepting nothing less than God's best. All I knew was that I always had a desire to own my home. I saved up for two years and was excited to make the purchase and settle down in my own space. Although it wasn't my ultimate desire, I was happy with the home I bought.

To make a long story short, I lived in that home less than a year. It had hidden issues such a faulty foundation, a water flow issue with the external drain system and was not in the best neighborhood or location. When I had to relocate due to work and sell the house, it would not sell as the price I paid for it. This was in 2008, so the housing market was extremely volatile that year. I was one of the people caught in the housing crash with a home I overpaid for that would not sell for full price, or even a short sale. I ended up doing a Deed-in-lieu of foreclosure, which I didn't know at the time has all the same credit reporting and loan penalty ramification as a regular foreclosure. My credit took a major hit and I was ineligible to apply for a home loan for three years following the date the mortgage company reported the foreclosure, not the date the foreclosure actually took place. This added an additional two years to my waiting period. I had to wait five full years before I could buy a home again. Yet, the desire of home ownership never left my heart.

During this season, I experienced a supernatural spiritual transformation and started my amazing relationship with Christ. I learned to pray, hear from God, live by faith, and never settle. I also learned to believe God for the impossible. So, although the banks would not give me a home loan, I believe I heard from God that I would get non-traditional financial assistance or loan. My good friend is a realtor and she calls this "creative financing". I received specifics in prayer about letters I should write and people I should reach out to requesting creative financing. I looked at homes, worked with realtors and continued to apply (unsuccessfully) for a traditional bank loan. I even found a home I wanted to build, went to the plot of land on a regular basis, prayed over it, called it forth into my possession and decreed the Word of God that everywhere my feet tread upon God would give me and my territory would be enlarged. I did all of these things because I felt that I had heard from God, coupled with my desire, and it was absolutely his will.

However, no matter what I did, nothing was working. Over the course of time, I worked through four of the checkpoints below and discovered the fifth during the process. You see, I wanted my own home so badly. It was one of my greatest desires next to getting married and having children. The seed of home ownership was planted in me at a young age and I just knew this was my season. After about a year of many failed efforts, I learned another valuable lesson:

It does not matter how much you want something, God's best will only manifest in His divine timing.

GOD'S TIMING...NOT YOURS

I was not able to buy or build a home in that season. Now, a few years later I live in a different state and am writing this book from the beautiful rose gold and turquoise accented cream decorated living room of my second home. This home is truly the desire of my heart. I did not have to make any compromises. The price even fits my budget in a very comfortable manner. The purchase process was extremely simple, everything flowed almost effortlessly. The ease in acquiring this home, the desire of my heart home confirms another valuable lesson learned in hearing from God:

God's best will flow effortlessly, with peace and you will not have to compromise or settle in what you desire from God.

During the previous season I was a mature follower of Christ and was sure I had heard from God, but confused about why things were not aligning with what I heard. The fact was that I did hear from God, but I did not get the corresponding instructions moving forward. Indeed, God wanted me to purchase a home. He wanted me to do it in his timing, however. When I heard from him in prayer, it was my season of preparation, not of manifestation. I was receiving a Word from God concerning my future; and he was planting a vision in my heart coupled with the desire he already placed there as well. This is why it is imperative to gain further instructions once the Lord speaks to you. You must hear from God concerning timing and at the very least, gain his wisdom for the next step you need to take.

This is what causes most single women to get frustrated, anxious, and impatient concerning their future husband. You know that God has placed this desire in your heart. Yet you begin to question if the desire is God given because of the time that is passing without the manifestation of your greatest desire. You have even tried compromising or trying to "work with" and accept certain men you normally would not have any interest in. You ignore red flags and deal breakers, compromise on your standards and values and still end up alone and sometimes heartbroken. After all your efforts and testing the waters, even with your relationship with God by being disobedient and ignoring his Word, it still has not produced your husband. More years fly by and you are still unmarried. Be encouraged, sis. Just like with my home purchase. Even though it has not happened in your timing does not mean it is not going to happen. It does not mean that you have heard from God incorrectly. It simply means that:

The vision and desire God has given you is for the future. This is a season of preparation, not of manifestation.

The key is to hear from God and gather the next steps you need to take in your current season. However the Lord leads you is exactly how he wants you to prepare to receive the vision in your due season of manifestation.

NOTES, THOUGHTS AND REFLECTIONS

Chapter 7
CLARITY AND CONFIRMATION: THE FIVE CHECKPOINTS

CHECKPOINT #1: THE SPOKEN WORD OF GOD

We should all hear the still small voice of God. The Bible says, "My sheep know My Voice." Even if the Lord does not speak to you in all the ways I listed previously, you should always be able to hear His Voice, the spoken Word of God. When you hear from God either through spiritual discernment, a vision or dream, a Word of Knowledge or Word of Wisdom, these are confirmed and clarity is given when the Lord speaks directly to your heart. This is also a good checkpoint if someone comes and shares something they believe the Lord has revealed to them about your life. The first thing that you should do, is go into prayer and listen for the Lord's voice. Remember, you can discern whether it's your voice, the Lord's voice or the voice of enemy because of two requirements: Love and Authority. If you sense love but no authority, it could be your own voice and thoughts running through your mind. If you sense authority or hear a word or phrase that seems "empty", "dry" or "powerless" it could be the enemy. But, when you can sense love, comfort, and kindness, coupled with authority, power, and might, you know that is the Great God Jehovah speaking to your heart and spirit. If you are still unsure, move on the next Checkpoint. The good thing is that the Checkpoints check each other. Whenever you are unsure or unclear, go to the next Checkpoint until your spirit has peace.

CHECKPOINT #2: THE WRITTEN WORD OF GOD

Everything that we do is based on the written Word of God. How we pray, how we hear from God, how we worship and how we live, is all based upon the directions, instructions and wisdom provided throughout the scriptures. One of the best ways to confirm what you have heard from God is by going to the scripture. The scripture is the foundation of our faith. The scripture also provides a source of clarity and background for what we are receiving. We use the stories within as examples and references for daily living.

Therefore, if someone professes to have the Spirit of God (Jesus Christ's Spirit) yet speaks things that directly oppose the Word of God; it is not of God and therefore is a false and deceiving spirit. If you receive a dream or vision that directly opposes or contradicts the Word of God, it is your own spirit or emotions and not the spirit of God leading you. There a lot of people with different opinions and beliefs in the world. I have found that during the dating process, it is highly important to find out what scriptural basis the men I am engaging with are basing their beliefs and lifestyle choices. If the scriptures are being twisted for personal benefit and pride, I question the validity. In addition, remember the two highlights I made earlier. Any interpretation of the Word, should always be rooted in the love of God and fulfill the Great Commission.

I have an example of how I was deceived one season with a man I should have never entered into a relationship with. I was flourishing spiritually and naturally in my life, I was at a really great place. There was a friend I was semi-close to and I decided perhaps I was being too picky and should give him a chance. I went into prayer and I heard two words. Normally, when the Lord speaks to me I hear a full sentence, phrase or paragraph, never just two words. I also didn't recognize these words as anything I ever studied or read in the Word, but I hear people saying it in the world a lot. I knew to check the scriptures first and foremost. I went to the Word and couldn't find those words, nor could I find any principle that alluded to the belief system those words are based upon.

Try as I might, I could not find a biblical basis for what I was hearing. This was also the season God taught me about how to discern his voice form the voice of the enemy. The enemy was giving me this word to deceive me into thinking me and this friend were somehow meant to be together and distract me from fulfilling my purpose. I knew this wasn't God speaking to me after I searched the Word and realized there was no presence of love in the words being spoken to me. But, I wanted love so badly, I chose to go against what I knew in my heart was not a good relationship decision and got involved with this person. It ended horribly, I was distracted and thrown completely off for two full years as a result of this decision to follow a foreign voice with words I could not confirm using scripture.

CHECKPOINT #3: THE PEACE OF GOD

> And let the peace (soul harmony which comes) from Christ rule (act as umpire continually) in your hearts [deciding and settling with finality all questions that arise in your minds, in that peaceful state] to which as [members of Christ's] one body you were also called [to live]. And be thankful (appreciative), [giving praise to God always].
> *Colossians 3:15 Amplified Bible, Classic Edition (AMPC)*

This scripture tells us how powerful our inner peace is in making life decisions. Sometimes when we are unsure which option is best or which direction we need to take, our peace can guide us wonderfully coupled with the leadership of the Holy Spirit. If you have not heard from God yet, or what you are hearing or seeing is conflicting with the peace in your Spirit that is a major signal in what choice to make. Wisdom is being able to listen to the voice of God and follow your peace.

Sometimes you may wonder if you are hesitating because of lack of peace or another negative emotion such as anxiety, frustration, worry, stress or nervousness. Peace is greater than a temporary emotion you are experiencing. It comes from deep within your hear or spirit. Even though you can be nervous about a change that will take place or the future once you move on what is God is telling you to do, you should still have an inner peace. If you truly can not tell, take moment to yourself. Get quiet before the Lord. Clear your thoughts. Hone in on your peace. It is not difficult to tell when you do and do not have peace. I have found that most people simply do not WANT to make the decision or change. Wrestling with God is different than not having peace.

The Google definition of peace is freedom from war or violence. War and violence are strong words. You can sense whether you are experiencing war or violence in your spirit or simply hesitation or nervousness. The lack of peace is as if your spirit and mind is in turmoil. There is no rest, no calmness and no quiet. When you hear from God, you will also sense peace within your spirit for the things the Lord is speaking or revealing to you.

CHECKPOINT #4: WISE COUNCIL

The Bible says there is safety in the multitude of counsel in Proverbs 15:22. In other words, don't go at life and make major decisions alone. Talking to others about what you have heard or seen from the Spirit of God is a tricky checkpoint that must be coupled with the others, it should never stand on its own. If you do not run it pass the other checkpoints you could open yourself up to manipulation or deceit, intentionally or unintentionally. Therefore, you must have already verified using the written Word of God, spoken Word of God and the peace of God. It can be helpful if you are struggling with recognizing peace to talk it over with wise council. I have found that during the conversation they can sense or discern beyond my words and thoughts and speak directly to my situation. It is very helpful because you can talk in a safe place and gain another perspective, especially when your emotions seem intense and overwhelming.

There are Three Keys to determining what actually is wise council versus someone else's opinion, philosophy, or judgement of you and your situation:

1) The person must be filled with AND led by the Holy Spirit. Unfortunately, there are many believers that are filled with the Holy Spirit, yet they are not submitted to his leadership for their lives. You will see the fruit of the Spirit as well as the natural fruit of that person's faith walk and this will help you determine if they are truly led by the Holy Spirit. If the person is not led by God's Spirit, how can you expect them to speak into your life with godly wisdom? They will not be able to flow with the Holy Spirit and minister to you, if they do not flow with the Holy Spirit in their own life.

2) The person must have a pure heart and pure intentions towards you and preferably praying for you regularly. This type of person wants nothing but the best for you and has no ulterior motives. They will not be seeking a personal agenda or to further their own philosophy or beliefs. When you seek them for help it will be coming from a pure and well intentioned place that you can trust.

3) The person must be WISE. In other words, they must have operational insight as expressed in their own life. Similar to being led by the Holy Spirit, this person must have the fruit of being a wise person in order to be considered wise council. For example, if you need help with God leading you on a financial matter, you wouldn't go to someone who struggles financially. They can try to tell you what to do, but their very belief system and knowledge has landed them in position of financial struggle. Taking their council, your situation will soon follow theirs.

No matter what the person tells you, make sure you run it pass the Word of God and your inner peace. If the guidance they give leaves you confused or feeling even more unrest, go with the last thing you heard from God yourself. At one time I was making a major life decision and thought I could talk to my good girlfriend who used to give me great advice in times past. I was not concerned with her present spiritual state, I was trusting God and not judging her recent lifestyle choices that were leading her away from God. I still considered her my friend and I knew she had lots of Bible knowledge. However, in the conversation when I asked her about this major life choice, her advice was off. As she was speaking, it was if I was being hit with bricks in my spirit. I did not have peace with a single word she was saying. She ended the conversation with a story about her own situation and what her decisions had been. I realized after I hung up the phone that her advice was not coming from a pure and free place, but was based solely on her past experience. She was not led by God in that moment and although I considered her a source of wise council, I learned in that moment she could no longer be wise council for me because of her present spiritual state. The fruit of her life revealed she was disconnected from God. She was not being led by God in that current season of her life and therefore she could not be led of God in giving me godly, wisdom filled advice.

CHECKPOINT #5: THE "NATURAL" WILL LINE UP

I learned about checkpoint number four when I first heard God tell me to purchase a home the second time around. I saw in the Word that the Lord would enlarge my territory and that he would also give me the desires of my heart. I had much peace about moving forward. I got plenty of wise council that home buying was the best choice to make if you were financial capable. Yet and still, after months of taking unconventional measures to secure "creative financing" (the terminology of my dear realtor friend), I was unable to obtain the financing I needed. The credit reporting of my first home foreclosure in addition to the current state of the real estate industry, which was still recovering from the hit of '08, was hindering my ability to obtain any form of financing, creative or not.

I went to the assistant pastor of my church to get some personalized wise council from one of the smartest and biblically astute men I knew. I told him how I had followed all the checkpoints of confirming what I heard from God, yet things still were not working out. I was confused, yet I knew in my heart that the Lord wanted me to buy a second home. I knew that it was His Will for my life to be a successful home owner.

As I went on about my previous home and what I was doing in this season to obtain "creative financing", he listened quietly and intently. Then, he calmly replied, "Well, Sarita, the other thing you need to realize is that when God is leading you to do something, things in the natural will also line up." And he left it there. Short and sweet, yet powerful indeed. He was right. I understood exactly what he meant and in that moment my spirit was at rest with his words. I went home, prayed and realized it was not that I had misheard from God, but it was not the proper timing of God to manifest this vision that he had laid upon my heart.

Faith without works is dead. You hear from God and then take action with what God has revealed to your heart. Yet, at a certain point, things should begin lining up in the natural world with what you believe you have heard supernaturally in the spirit. There is balance between having the grace of God and peacefully moving forward in action (works), and striving with sweat and tears with no manifestation of the things you pray for.

This is why it is important to not only hear from God concerning his vision and plans for your life, but also to hear from God concerning timing and current focus. He may sometimes reveal his desire for your future so that you can begin preparing in the present, as was the case in my personal example. The Lord revealed to me his desire, which also matched my heart's desire. This was not a season of manifestation, but instead, it was my season of preparation. I needed to prepare seven more years to acquire the home, which was exactly what I wanted, with ease, no compromises, and favor abounding throughout the process. In addition, I moved to another state during the preparation season. Although I thought I was to settle down and serve that city, the Lord had a much greater plan in store for my future, for me to serve and launch my business/ministry in the city I currently reside.

JOURNALING CLARITY AND CONFIRMATION

God is not the author of confusion. The wonderful thing about the checkpoints listed is that the checkpoints check each other. When in doubt, simply follow the last clear instruction given and follow your peace. The Lord will not allow you, his precious daughter to wander aimlessly and in confusion. He wants you to hear, receive and submit to His leadership and experience the most blessed single season possible. Below is a daily prayer for you to pray over the next seven days straight as you begin gaining clarity and confirmation of what you are hearing from God. I have also included some space for you to write out your thoughts and what you believe God is beginning to reveal or speak to you over the next seven days. You can also pair this book with The Single Woman's Prayer Journal to keep track of prayers over the next 52 weeks. Remember, God's word comes to direct, teach, comfort, build, encourage and give understanding. As much as you want to hear from him, he wants you to receive your answers directly from heaven as well. As you begin to document what the Lord is saying to you, it will become clearer and your relationship with God will grow.

The Single Woman's Prayer

FATHER,
I PRAY THAT YOU WILL BEGIN TO SPEAK TO MY HEART IN THIS SEASON LIKE NEVER BEFORE. MAKE MY SPIRIT SENSITIVE TO YOUR SPIRIT AND HELP ME TO RECEIVE YOUR LEADERSHIP AND GUIDANCE FOR MY SINGLE SEASON. SHOW ME WHAT YOU WOULD HAVE ME TO FOCUS ON DURING THIS SEASON SO THAT I MAY GROW SPIRITUALLY, EMOTIONALLY, MENTALLY, AND NATURALLY. REVEAL TO ME THE PURPOSE FOR WHICH YOU HAVE CREATED ME, SO THAT I MAY BEGIN TO FOCUS AND FLOW IN THIS PURPOSE. I THANK YOU FOR PREPARING MY FUTURE HUSBAND FOR ME, AS YOU PREPARE ME FOR HIM. GIVE ME AN ABUNDANCE OF WISDOM FOR DATING AND STARTING NEW FRIENDSHIPS WITH MEN. HELP ME NOT TO RUSH OR BE ANXIOUS BUT TO GET TO KNOW THEM IN THE DATING/COURTING PROCESS WHILE LISTENING FOR YOUR LEADERSHIP ALONG THE WAY. GIVE ME STRENGTH AND THE SPIRIT OF OBEDIENCE TO SUBMIT TO YOUR GUIDANCE AND LEADERSHIP THROUGHOUT THIS SEASON. REMOVE ALL CONFUSION AND CLUTTER THAT WOULD TRY TO DETER ME FROM YOUR PERFECT WILL.
IN JESUS' NAME, AMEN.

NOTES & THOUGHTS

Day 1

Day 2

Day 3

Day 4

Day 5

Day 6

Day 7

Chapter 8
NEXT STEPS

Now that you have created or enhanced your prayer life, heard from the Lord, and received confirmation, your next step is to move forward in obedience. If you struggle with submitting and obeying God's will ask Him for strength. Pray in your Heavenly Prayer Language. God will give you whatever it is that you need to listen to him. Be encouraged that he will also accompany you along your journey, providing you with grace, anointing, favor, provision, strength, and love. You are not alone in your journey through life. God said he would never leave or forsake you. You do not have to be afraid or feel as if you are lacking in anything you need to take action with what God has shown you.

You do not have to wait until you have a husband to move forward. Your life is happening right now, sis, not only after you get married. Marriage is simply a season shift that takes place at God's divine timing. Until then, there is much significance to fulfill with your life. Even as you journey through relationships that may or may not work out with men, there is still great purpose for each and every season. God's best is ready for you take hold of right now in this season of singleness.

God's best is waiting on you to Start, Shift or Move

Take a small, but meaningful step forward. Just start. There is grace in simply starting. There is anointing in saying, yes. There is favor in obedience. There is a blessed future ahead in this season even as you wait on your husband to manifest.

Fear not, for I am with you; Be not dismayed, for I am your

God. I will strengthen you, Yes, I will help you, I will uphold you with My righteous right hand.

Isaiah 41:10 New King James Version (NKJV)

PART 3

PRAYERS FOR SELF AND FUTURE HUSBAND

Chapter 9
TOPICAL PRAYERS

Therefore, confess your sins to one another [your false steps, your offenses], and pray for one another, that you may be healed and restored. The heartfelt and persistent prayer of a righteous man (believer) can accomplish much [when put into action and made effective by God—it is dynamic and can have tremendous power].

James 5:16 Amplified Bible (AMP)

HOW TO USE THESE PRAYERS

I have intentionally created this section with exactly 21 prayers, as led by the Holy Spirit of course. As I was writing the prayers out of my heart, based on what I have experienced, seen or know to be much needed prayer for your own single season and as intercession for your future husband that you have yet to meet, I ended at exactly eleven prayers for the single woman and ten prayers of intercession for your future husband. As I asked God whether I should add more or even it out so there are eleven prayers each, I knew that 21 prayers was the divine number to include (I originally planned for 20 total).

Most of you know that 21 days represents a Daniel Fast found in the book of Daniel, chapter 10 versus 2-3. Daniel fasted specifically because he needed answers from heaven. The prayer was held up in a battle within the heavenly realm and the answer was released to Daniel after 21 days, God had the victory. Just like Daniel, you also need answers from heaven. You may even want to transform your single season as well. If you need breakthrough, deliverance or to grow spiritually, fasting and prayer is an extremely powerful process. Starve the flesh and feed the spirit. Meaning, discipline your body by removing those things that your flesh greatly enjoys, such as sweets, carbs and flavored beverages, or do a full-blown Daniel fast of only veggies, fruits and water. Simultaneously, feed your spirit with the Word of God. Pray daily, and in order, one of each of the provided prayers. This way the first eleven days you will focus solely on growing as a woman, then move on to interceding for your future husband the final ten days of the fast. Make sure you study the Word daily, in addition to praying daily during the 21 days. I recommend doing a topical study that corresponds with the topic of your prayer that day. You can also fast from TV, radio, and/or social media and put yourself in a spiritual bubble as Jesus and Moses did when they went away to the mountain to fast and pray. Jesus, Moses and Daniel each had a supernatural, life transforming encounter with God during their seasons of fasting which is a possible outcome for you as well.

Even though the quantity of prayers was created with fasting in mind, they are not only for seasons of fasting and praying. I want you to keep these prayers as tools to use when needed throughout your single season. You can rewrite, modify and add to the prayers so they can connect with you and your circumstances on a customized and deeper level. The prayers for your future husband can also be prayed over your male children, family members or brothers in Christ. I actually had not only my future husband in mind, but also my son and my natural brother in mind as I determined the topics and how the prayers should be written. When you start courting or become engaged to a man, you can pray these prayers over his life as well. The men need our intercession in this world we live in, now more than ever to take their rightful place in leadership within the Body of Christ in this generation.

Lastly, even if you don't have complete faith or you are sensing some internal doubt as you read these prayers, pray them out loud anyway. Your faith will grow and doubt will diminish as you pray, hear from God, study the Word and learn from spiritual teachers God places in your life. The key is simply to start and grow where you are. I am confident that these prayers will be a blessing to your life and to your future husband's life as well!

Topical Prayers for the Phenomenal Single Woman

HEARING FROM GOD PRAYER

Lord, I ask you to increase my hearing to your voice and help me to hear from you with great clarity. As I study your Word, allow it to speak directly to my heart by your Spirit. I thank you for never leaving or forsaking me, even when I make mistakes. I know that you are always speaking to me and I ask for guidance and clarity for/to _____. I thank you in advance, that I already have all the wisdom I need to make this decision and change I need to make. I ask for confirmation of your word with signs following. I know that you are not the author of confusion. I have great discernment and can distinguish between my voice, your voice and the voice of the enemy. I chose to submit and follow your voice and leadership only. In Jesus name, Amen.

PURPOSE PRAYER

Lord, reveal to me your purpose, plans and destiny for my life. Show me with great clarity what purpose I have been designed to fulfill. Give me direction on how to move forward towards this destiny and incorporate purpose-FULL living into my daily life. Surround me with a blessed support system who will encourage and inspire me towards greatness. Give me clarity for my calling for my present season and help my focus to be on godly purpose with destiny driven goals. As I begin walking and living in your purpose, allow fruit to flow and others' lives to be changed as confirmation that I am on the right path. Remove any obstacle and cancel every attack that works against the fulfillment of my godly purpose as I work towards it. In Jesus' name, Amen.

BECOMING THE BEST VERSION OF YOURSELF PRAYER

Father, I thank you for helping me to become the best version of myself spiritually, mentally, emotionally and naturally. I ask for wisdom and guidance of what lifestyle changes I need to make in order to fulfill your divine will for my life. I thank you in advance for the discipline I need to be the best steward over my finances, health, children, home, job, business and ministry. Continue to mold me daily into the Proverbs 31 woman you desire for me to be. I thank you that as I grow as a woman, I am also being prepared to be the best wife and mother I can be. Allow me to easily access every resource needed to grow and develop in this season. Surround me with supportive and loving women of God to encourage me in my personal, professional and spiritual growth. In Jesus' name, Amen.

UNGODLY COMPARISON PRAYER

Lord, help me to stop comparing myself to other women in an ungodly and unfruitful manner. Help me to rejoice with other women that are being blessed and not to judge them negatively. Help me also not to put myself down or beat myself up because I have not received the husband I have been praying for yet. Help me to keep my eyes on my own race and be inspired by others, not jealous or envious. Keep my heart close to you and strengthen my faith walk. Bless my season of singleness with great peace, joy and love so that I am whole, fulfilled and satisfied, even as I continue to stand in faith for your promise of a godly marriage.

PATIENCE PRAYER

Father, I ask for supernatural strength and peace in this season of waiting so that I may continue to be patient and wait on you to bring forth my KING. Remove all anxiety and feelings of despair from my heart and mind. Let your peace flow and fill me up with your love so that I do not experience any lack of love in my life. Open my eyes to see and receive your provision of love for my life even as a single woman. I thank you in advance for friendships, family, mentors and sisters who surround me with support, encouragement and love so that I never feel lonely or rushed. Help me to focus on your voice and guidance and not on the negative words of others concerning my singleness. In Jesus' name, Amen.

PRAYER FOR FUTURE HUSBAND

Father, I know that Psalm 37:4 is true and you want to bring me one of the greatest desires of my heart: my future husband. I pray that you are perfecting him in this season as you are perfecting me and we are both growing closer to Christ. Your Word says that if I have faith the size of a mustard seed, that I can ask and the Father in Heaven will do it. I thank you right now, for connecting me and my future husband and that we will have a blessed and purpose-FULL marriage. I pray that anything that may block, hinder or prevent him from finding me be swiftly removed. Reveal to me any blessing blockers that I may need to change in my own life, yet give me wisdom not to begin to "work for" or "earn" a husband by my own good works. Help me to trust in your divine timing and give my heart peace. Remove all stress, worry and anxiety in my heart and allow your grace for the single season to flow over me. Help me to rest in You, as I wait patiently and keep my focus on the things above. In Jesus name I pray, Amen.

WISDOM IN DATING PRAYER

Father, I ask for an abundance of wisdom in my dating season. Give me wisdom beyond my years so that I may make the decisions that you want me to make and am continually led by your Spirit. Increase my discernment and sensitivity to your voice and Spirit as I engage in forming new friendships with men in this season. Help me to guard my heart and protect my mind, while also being open to the love you desire to bring into my life. Help me to discern real, godly love from fake love. Connect me with the person you desire me to grow and build with and remove all distractions. Give me the strength I need to obey your leadership and focus on godly living while dating and courting. In Jesus' name, Amen.

RELATIONSHIP PRAYER

Lord, your Word says that you give wisdom to those who ask. I ask now for an abundance of wisdom regarding my relationship with _____. If it is your will for me to be with him or not I pray for confirmation and peace in a way that speaks directly to my heart. I know that you are not the author of confusion. I thank you, for directing my footsteps with _____ and making our paths straight. I thank you for the opportunity to get to know him better. I ask now that you continue to confirm which direction our relationship should take. If he is not for me I ask that you swiftly remove him from my life before my heart is intertwined. I thank you for your protection through your Word, wise counsel and the leading of your spirit. I also thank you for strength and wisdom in making the next decision that is in line with your perfect will. I pray that you help us to make good decisions concerning each other that are pleasing to you. In Jesus' name. Amen.

HEALING PRAYER

Lord, I know that you are Jehovah-Rapha, the God who heals me. You are also the mender of broken hearts. Please swiftly heal my heart, mind and spirit in this season so that I may receive and give love again in your timing. Help my life to align with your will so that peace and joy may freely flow throughout my days. Direct my footsteps forward on the path you have me to take in getting my life back on track. Take this pain, hurt, bitterness, shame, unforgiveness and guilt from me immediately. I believe I am set free in Christ and I thank you, Jesus for healing my heart. In Jesus' name, Amen.

DETACH FROM THE PAST PRAYER

Lord, I pray that you help me to stop replaying this story of past hurt, pain, mistakes and memories of _____ in my mind over and over again. I don't want to stay stuck in that place, I want to move forward in you and with you. Show me what you want me to focus my thoughts on. You said you would keep me at perfect peace if my mind is stayed on you. Speak to me with words and visions so that I may detach from my past and focus on my future. Show me what you would have me to re-focus on at this point in my life. Help me to flow in your peace throughout my day and keep my mind on you. In Jesus' name, Amen.

SELF-FORGIVENESS AND LETTING GO PRAYER

Father, I thank you for loving me so much that you do not remember my sin, past mistakes, disobedience, ignoring your voice, putting myself first, putting a relationship first, desiring a man more than I desired pleasing you or _____! You are a good, loving God who already knew the mistakes I would make in life before I made them, yet you still love me. You still have a plan and purpose for me to fulfill, you still see me as your perfect daughter! I forgive myself because you have forgiven me. I receive your forgiveness and forgive myself at the same time. Help me to walk in self-forgiveness and let go of the past. Help me to forget those things that are behind me and press forward towards the high calling you have for me in Christ Jesus! In Jesus' name. Amen.

Topical Intercessory Prayers for Future Husband

FOR HIS RELATIONSHIP WITH CHRIST

Lord, keep my future husband's heart close to you at all times. I ask that your angels guide and protect him so that he will never be pulled away from you. Teach him your voice and how to flow with your will for his life. Give him every confirmation he needs to rest assured that it is your Spirit leading and guiding him. Give him a spirit of obedience and submission to follow your leadership as you direct his footsteps. Bless his life with grace and peace as he walks with Christ in every area of his life. In Jesus' name, Amen.

FOR HIS IDENTITY IN CHRIST

Father, I pray that you help my future husband to find his identity in Christ only, not from the world, friends, family, or society. I pray that he can hear from your voice clearly and you alone define who he is as a man, father, brother, servant, friend, leader, and future husband. I pray that your Word has weight in his life and not the words of others or made up words in his own mind. Help him to discern guidance directly from heaven or satanic guidance trying to lead him astray. Draw his heart close to you and continue to direct his paths towards godliness. In Jesus' name, Amen.

FOR HIS PROTECTION

Father, protect my future husband from all physical and spiritual harm. Keep him safe and covered by your feathers. Help him to continually abide under the shadow of the Almighty, whose power no foe can withstand. I decree and declare that no weapon formed against him shall prosper and every tongue that rises against him, you shall condemn. Let every man that attacks his character or accuses him falsely be shown to be a liar. Keep his mind strong and bless with an abundance of mental agility to overcome any attack on his heart, mind, or spirit. Keep him safe and close to you at all times and let your hand never be removed from his life. In Jesus' name, Amen.

FOR HIS FOCUS

Father, I pray that you keep my future husband's focus on Christ and not on the things of this world. Help him not to become distracted, a lover of money or enticed by the things this world offers that are not pleasing in your eyes. Allow his heart to remain in your hands and his eyes to be fixed on the Kingdom agenda you have planned for his life. Give him wisdom to recognize counterfeit plans and options so that he will not be distracted but can remain disciplined and focused on godly purpose. In Jesus' name, Amen.

FOR HIS STRENGTH

Lord, I pray that you give my future husband supernatural strength in his single season. Help him not to succumb to the desires of the flesh or the pride of life, chasing money or women. Also, strengthen his mind when facing challenges of this world and the weight of the responsibility he has presently in his life. Remind him that you are his Helper and that your grace is sufficient for him when he needs Heaven's help. Surround him with high quality, Spirit filled and Spirit-led men who can encourage him on his path of godly living. In Jesus' name, Amen.

FOR HIS HEART AND SPIRIT

Father, I ask that you will keep my future husbands heart, mind and spirit close to you. Cover his life with the blood of Jesus protection so that every attack the enemy sends his way will not succeed. Allow your grace to cover and protect him, even when he makes poor choices in life. Always bring Him back to your presence, draw him by your Spirit. Mold his heart into the loving heart you desire him to have. Build his character into the strong leader and high priest of his home that you have called him to be. Allow nothing to tear him apart from you. I pray his relationship with you grows stronger and stronger. In Jesus's name, Amen.

FOR HIS GODLY LIFESTYLE

Father, I pray that my future husband's lifestyle is pleasing to you. Help him to tap into the strength and discipline that lives on the inside of his spirit to live according to your Word, which is your will for his life. Guide him in making the best decisions for his life and bless the works of his hands. Help him never to become a lover of money, a chaser of success without godliness, a mis-manager of women's hearts or a rebellious soul. Keep his lifestyle in line and in agreement with how you would have him to live as kingdom minded man in the earth. In Jesus' name, Amen.

FOR HIS LEADERSHIP

Father, I pray that you will continue to mold my future husband into the godly leader you have created him to be. Draw him by your Spirit and give him a hunger and thirst after righteousness. Allow his desire to be for Your will and Your purpose only. Help him to find his identity in Christ Jesus and teach him how to lead in this family, community and ministry. Connect him with another godly leader that can hold him accountable and teach him the love of God in word and in deed. Give him wisdom beyond his years so that he may lead men, women and children in every area of his life with grace, ease and fruitfulness. In Jesus' name, Amen.

FOR HIS RELATIONSHIPS AND COVERING

Lord, I pray that you are connecting my future husband with other godly men. Surround him with a high quality, high caliber support system and male role models. Allow his leadership to be men who are filled with and led by your spirit with fruit abounding on their lives. Expose him to kingdom minded men that live an attractive and godly lifestyle. I pray that this support system and leadership will be the godly covering he needs in his life as a single man and also as a husband. Give his wisdom to discern between the proper friendships and relationships to invest in and move forward with. In Jesus' name, Amen.

FOR HIS MENTAL AGILITY

Lord, I pray that you keep my future husband's mind strong and agile. Help him not be led astray by the spirit of error, but to only follow sound doctrine of Jesus Christ. I come against the spirit of confusion that tries to twist scriptures and cause dissention. I pray that my future husband is filled with and led by Your Spirit only and has wisdom to discern the difference between true and false teachings. Help him to learn and grow in the love of God based on the Word of God. I pray that his relationship with you grows stronger and stronger all the days of his life. In Jesus' name, Amen.

About the Author

Sarita A. Foxworth is a certified Christian Life Coach. Her life's work is to help people of God pray, hear from God and obtain the blessed families they desire. She provides biblical prayer based life coaching through group coaching programs, luxury life coaching retreats and global speaking tours.

Her literary works include:

The Single Woman's Prayer Book:
How to Get Answers from Heaven

How to Heal a Broken Heart:
Transition from Pain to Peace

How to Prepare for Your Future Husband:
Waiting, Dating and Trusting God for Your Adam

Giving Birth to Miracles:
Manifesting Supernatural Childbirth

The Prophetic Woman:
Boldly Declaring the Word of the Lord

"My goal is to help you to hear from God, flow with God and manifest what he desires for your life"- *Sarita A. Foxworth*

To book Sarita as a guest speaker at your next event visit

www.Saritafoxworth.com

and fill out the contact us form. To attend a live online or in person event join Sarita's mailing list.